T0158602

HOOK

The idea behind why ideas catch on

Pat Langton

First published 2021 by Wilkinson Publishing Pty Ltd
ACN 006 042 173
Wilkinson Publishing
PO Box 24135, Melbourne, VIC 3001, Australia
Ph: +61 3 9654 5446
enquiries@wilkinsonpublishing.com.au
www.wilkinsonpublishing.com.au

Cover and book design by Pat Langton.
Printed and bound in Australia by Ligare Pty Ltd.

ISBN: 9781925927597

A catalogue record for this book is available from the National Library of Australia.

Follow Wilkinson Publishing on social media and tell us about your great Hook.

Contents

Prelude, I think it's called.

Firstly, I want to thank my wife for believing in me to write this book. I'm passionate about messages and communication but without her support this would never have happened. Secondly, I want to thank every book I've ever read, each and every one has had an enormous impact on what I've done in my career and what is in this book.

There are some people I want to thank that don't even know me, that I have never met and may never meet: Rory Sutherland, Thomas Kemeny, Jim Aitchison (one of the first books I read), Dave Trott, Bob Hoffman, John Hegarty, Malcolm Gladwell, Simon Sinek, Luke Sullivan, Seth Godin, Richard Shotton. Each of these people have had an impact on my life in some form or another, and I'd recommend reading their books even before you read mine.

Their books are remarkable (stole this from Seth Godin) and they all have incredible insights into communication and human behaviour.

Thanks,

Me.

Introduction

The 'Hook' theory is an acronym. Okay, so you're probably thinking, oh no, not another acronym in marketing! Well, yes, sorry but this one actually is worth using, it has purpose and will help your marketing for the better. Hook (Human, Ownable, Offer & Keep), has been devised from years of research, reading hundreds of marketing books, studying thousands of campaigns, and personally working on hundreds of marketing campaigns.

It's been created like a textbook, so when you're creating your own marketing campaign you can use it as a guide to know if your campaign ticks all the boxes.

It's broken down into four simple words that, as a marketer, you can take with you, use and refer to when needed.

If your advertising has all four of these things you're onto a winner; three and it'll be very good; two you might just get away with it and with one you maybe should go back to the drawing board.

After years of creating thousands of campaigns, learning from some of the best campaigns, and making mistakes, there seemed to be a few common threads.

All these campaigns had elements of the Hook theory, some had all of them and some a few but all followed a similar theme.

Each chapter will focus on a word in the Hook acronym, breaking it down with stories and examples of how they have worked in the past and how each word can be used to create engaging campaigns that your audience will love.

This book will try to give you a simple formula to create great marketing campaigns. A great idea can come from anywhere, whether it's from an agency or brand, a great idea is a great idea.

There are many reasons why some campaigns are more successful than others, or why some stories catch on more than others.

A great idea can come from anywhere, whether it's from an agency or brand, a great idea is a great idea.

The Dollar Shave Club story is one that all content creators live by and refer to, not only did it shock the business world and sell a business for one billion dollars to Unilever, but they started with a film that was truly unique and spoke to their audience in a way that the industry had never done.

The story goes that in early 2010, Michael Dubin was at a Christmas party and was asked by one of his father's friends if he could help sell 250,000 razors he had gotten from Asia. Now this would usually raise a red flag but this sparked an idea in Michael that would change not only the razor industry but create an entirely new industry called 'direct subscription'. He thought, what if we sold razors for $1 each and they ended up at your door every month? You know, take on Gillette right, easy!

Now, before I go further, there is a back story that needs to be stated. Dubin was a comedian before Dollar Shave Club. In fact, while living in New York City from 2001 to 2010, he studied improvisational comedy for eight years with the legendary Upright Citizens Brigade.

This takes nothing away from what happened in 2012 when Dollar Shave Club uploaded their commercial to YouTube starring Michael Dubin himself. You see, Dublin understood human emotions and what his company offered was unique; they owned a marketplace and boy was that commercial something for their target market to take away and keep.

The film starts with Dubin sitting in an office and speaking directly to the camera. He introduces himself as 'Mike, founder of Dollar Shave Club' and goes on and says, 'Are our blades any good? No, our blades are fucking great.'

It was well written, smart, clever, funny and well crafted. The film instantly went viral, the company received more than 12,000 orders in the first 48 hours and it's now clocked over 26 million views on YouTube. If you haven't seen it, it's worth a watch.

Not bad considering it's a 1 minute and 30-second film. It's the perfect example that your audience isn't concerned about the length but making the film great offers them something to take away and potentially tell others.

The point of telling you that story is there's a formula to making your marketing/advertising great and this book will break it down using examples of great campaigns and even just simple ideas that have had an impact on all of us.

Hooks exist in all walks of life; a great pop song will have that 'hook' which resonates with people, TV shows and movies have hooks depending on the genre — mysteries, challenge or tragedy — that hook you in.

In order for your brand to succeed, the Hook theory gives you the ingredients to ensure you can create great films, posters, radio, social, digital, AR, AI or WTF other platforms are available to you.

As the world of marketing gets increasingly confusing with all the platforms we now have available to us, the more vital it is to make great advertising to stand out from the clutter.

In this book, we'll look at major campaigns and ideas from around the world that went 'viral', even before 'viral' was a concept. Ideas spread all the time but there are usually a few elements that give them that hook that gets them going.

Hooks exist in all walks of life; a great pop song will have that 'hook' which resonates with people, TV shows and movies have hooks depending on the genre — mysteries, challenge or tragedy — that hook you in.

So, it only makes sense that these hooks can work for marketing.

This book has been put together so you can unlock the true potential of your marketing campaigns. We will look at industries and campaigns that have been hugely successful by using these four principles.

I've broken it down into the simplest and easiest way to remember, so when you're creating your next campaign you can refer to the Hook theory and make sure your campaign has every chance of succeeding.

Think about this book as 'Marketing for smarties' as opposed to dummies.

As the world of marketing gets increasingly confusing with all the platforms we now have available to us, the more vital it is to make great advertising to stand out from the clutter.

Chapter 1: Human

“

Once you think of communication as entertainment rather than an ad or marketing, it changes the way you communicate to your audience.

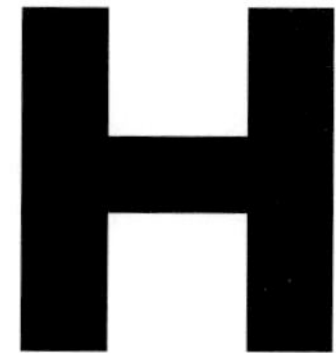uman emotion is a powerful tool when it comes to communications and storytelling.

There's a reason why Netflix is spending 11 billion dollars on content this year. We are emotional beings and we want to be entertained.

Netflix understands that humans respond to emotional storytelling, whether that be comedy, drama or mystery.

Once you think of communication as entertainment rather than an ad or marketing, it changes the way you communicate to your audience. The more they're entertained the more they're likely to remember you as a brand.

Psychology plays a huge role in marketing.

Human behaviour is the basis of all decision making. People think they're in control of the decisions that they make but science says otherwise. We are sheep, we tend to do things because others do them.

The perfect case of people being sheep is market research. David Ogilvy said it best, 'People don't think how they feel, they don't say what they think and they don't do what they say'.

Ogilvy's quote says a lot about humans, we're a funny bunch. We have a tendency to care what others think, so we adapt our thoughts to our environment.

Humans are the ones that make things 'go viral', not the media or platform. If you can resonate with humans then your message will spread. Sounds simple, right?

In November 2012, a campaign was created that has now become the most awarded and one of the most viral campaigns of all time. That campaign was 'Dumb Ways To Die' for Metro Trains in Melbourne, Australia.

At the time they weren't known outside of the city of Melbourne (why would they be?), and even then they had never done a public safety message before.

They could have gone down the path of gore or scare tactics (either of which would be perfectly logical strategies) but they went with comedy.

Comedy in a train safety campaign is a hook to begin with, it's unexpected and for the viewer it automatically gets their attention.

For those who don't know the ad, it opens on a cute, animated character running towards us, his head is on fire, a folky type song starts with lyrics that describe what we are seeing as the singer sings about dumb ways people die.

This ad taps into a simple human truth, that people generally aren't scared of dying, but they definitely don't want their friends to think they are stupid. So 'Dumb Ways To Die' is the perfect formula to address that.

This coupled with a catchy tune, cute animation and of course comedy made this popular with not only their target market (teens) but with almost everyone.

As it stands this campaign has generated over 185 million views on YouTube. McCann, the agency responsible, estimated that within two weeks it had generated at least $50 million worth of global media value in addition to more than 700 media stories, for a fraction of the cost of one TV ad.

'People don't think how they feel, they don't say what they think and they don't do what they say.'

– David Ogilvy

“

People don’t know what they want. Tell them what they want.

Human: Standing Out

Standing out, that's the point, isn't it? All humans try to stand out in some form or another, whether it's the clothes you wear, the tattoos you may have, the music you listen to or even the way you do your hair ... if you have any. These are the things that make you you and make you stand out. We're all trying to advertise, whether we like it or not.

Nature is a perfect example of standing out; look at the peacock that wants to mate or a flower that wants to be pollinated, these are nature's ways of standing out. And if they don't find a mate or get pollinated then they don't get noticed and eventually ... well ... die.

These simple analogies can be practised when we talk about brands. If they don't stand out or differentiate themselves from their competition then that brand will die.

There's a great story that there are two men walking in the desert and they come across a pack of dingos. They both start running but one man stops and starts putting on his runners. The other man says, 'What are you doing? You're not going to outrun those dingos'. He looks up at his mate and says, 'I don't need to outrun those dingos, I just need to outrun you'.

Brutal, yes, but the moral of the story is clear, you just need to be smarter than your competitors. Simple, right? Yes and no.

There are many ways to outsmart the competition but most importantly it's making sure your product is better than theirs or, if not, to stand out through advertising.

Advertising is all about standing out, and there are a lot of techniques to do that. Whether it's a great headline, activation or an amazing film/TV/social video, depending on what you want to call it these days. These are the things that will make a brand stand out over another, but advertising will only ever sell something once, if the product is shit, consumers won't come back.

Your advertising needs to come from a human insight, once you have that insight you'll stand out to your audience as it becomes relatable.

If people think it's worth something then people will want it.

Rory Sutherland tells a great story about potatoes, it goes like this. Frederick the Great, of Prussia, wanted his country to adopt potatoes as their primary crop. But people thought potatoes looked ugly, tasted funny, and farmers had no desire to grow them.

Frederick realised the farmers would rather be jailed than forced to grow potatoes. So he took a new approach and decided to re-brand the potato — changing its perceived value. He declared that potatoes were only for the royal, grew them in his garden, protected around the clock by his guards. People started to think if it's worth guarding then it's worth stealing. Not long after, people gathered to create an underground potato market.

This is a perfect example of playing on 'human emotions' as a technique to stand out. If people think it's worth something then people will want it.

Again, there are lots of techniques to stand out but the first is getting your product to a point of excellence and then letting the advertising do the rest. It's one thing having a good product and another letting people know you exist.

Doing business without advertising is like winking at a girl in the dark, you know what you're doing but nobody else does. That's another great quote by Stuart Brit, there are loads of them and they all make too much sense. But what we have to keep in mind, always, is the power of a brand and the power of the product they sell, because in every case if the product is good, they will come, talk and promote it for you. But if they don't know about it, they never will and it will take years to reach them.

Standing out is everything. The famous, now worldwide, agency BBH lives by it. Their logo is a black sheep and it came from their famous ad campaign for Levi's, where they simply showed a black sheep walking in the opposite direction to the rest of the white sheep with the line, 'when the world zigs, zag', to promote black jeans in the UK.

Now there are two things that made this great, that black jeans were a new, amazing, different product from Levi's, and the ad was simply awesome. The fact they didn't show a pair of jeans must have freaked out the marketing department but to their credit they ran it and it was hugely successful.

The reason brands don't stand out has a lot to do with being too involved with their product, they see their product and the product benefits as amazing and want to tell the world the specific details of that product. What they don't see is nobody really cares; people really care only about why you do what you do and if it's relatable to them.

A human insight is one of the main tools to get your brand into the consumers' minds. If you can relate to your customer they will relate to you.

“

A human insight is one of the main tools to get your brand into the consumers’ minds. If you can relate to your customer they will relate to you.

Human: Creativity

The good old Oxford Dictionary defines creativity as 'The use of imagination or original ideas to create something; inventiveness'.

Now, by looking at that, anyone with an imagination is creative. Right?

Creativity is the only thing that separates us from the rest of the animals.

There are many ways of being 'creative' and it's not just painting, making music — or in my case working in advertising.

There's a great story that shows the use of creativity in business, so good, in fact, that I hear they're about to make it into a Hollywood movie.

In 1946, Earl Silas Tupper began selling his plastic containers with spill-proof, airtight lids to department stores and hardware stores. They even had the idea of including them as giveaways with cigarettes. But despite winning awards for design, sales were bad, due to the reputation of plastic. The value of these plastic containers needed to be demonstrated.

Sales turned around with a simple creative business idea called Tupperware parties. They were the brainchild of a sales executive called Brownie Wise. Tupperware parties took off all around America and Mr Tupper eventually sold that company for $16 million — a fortune in those days — and the rest is history. Indeed, it started a whole new industry — 'Party Plan' — which provided much needed independence and financial security for thousands of women.

Unfortunately for Brownie Wise she fell out with the company owner, who was jealous of her growing celebrity, and she was written out of the company history. But her creative concept lives on today not just with Tupperware but a huge variety of products. Her creativity had a dramatic worldwide effect.

Her idea was not a beautifully written song, amazing painting or a great creative TV commercial, it was simply a great use of creativity to solve a problem that tapped into the target market for that product.

This type of creativity is within us all, and often it's more about recognising it than trying to force it to happen. Humans do creative things every day and don't even know it.

Whether it's a creative business plan or a poem you've written, the two are one and the same.

Often, this creativity is found most obviously in the people who are on your business's front line.

For example: a toothpaste factory had a problem. They sometimes shipped empty toothpaste boxes without the tube inside. They decided to hire an external engineering company to solve their problem. By using a high-tech precision scale it would sound a bell and flash lights whenever a toothpaste box weighed less than it should. The line would stop, someone would walk over, remove the defective box and then press another button to restart the line.

‘Creativity is the last unfair advantage we’re legally allowed to take over our competitors.’

As a result of the new package monitoring process, no empty boxes would be shipped out of the factory.

So they installed the gear, and with no more customer complaints about empty boxes the CEO felt the $8 million the equipment had cost was well spent. He then reviewed the line statistics report and discovered the number of empty boxes picked up by the scale in the first week was consistent with projections. Yay! But then in the next three weeks the stoppages were zero! Was the expensive new equipment faulty?

Puzzled, the CEO travelled down to the factory.

Just ahead of the new $8 million dollar solution sat a $20 desk fan blowing any empty boxes off the belt and into a bin. 'Oh, that,' the supervisor commented: 'Bert, the kid from maintenance, put it there because he was tired of walking over to restart the line every time that bloody bell rang.'

If only someone had asked the kid from maintenance before they spent eight million, eh?

Now this is not to absolutely try to devalue creativity — quite the opposite — it's trying to empower people to embrace it and recognise it. Knowing when something or someone is truly creative is an art in itself.

As Bill Bernbach said, 'Creativity is the last unfair advantage we're legally allowed to take over our competitors'.

Creativity is your edge and humans own it. So use it next time you need to solve a problem.

“

Your advertising should talk to your audience, not yell at them.

Human: Behaviour

The study of human behaviour now has a name, it's 'behavioural economics', which studies the effects of psychological, cognitive, emotional, cultural decision making of individuals and how their decisions can vary from the classic rationale theory.

Behavioural Economics is playing a bigger role in marketing than ever before, marketers are trying to find new ways to understand the consumer.

A simple example of how a small change in how we describe a product or service can have a huge influence on the decision made by the buyer.

For example, if you offered two t-shirts to a potential buyer, one that said 'made from cotton' and the other said 'made from Egyptian cotton', you could make the assumption that the buyer may choose the latter, and potentially you charge him/her $20 more for the privilege.

The point is small changes in how you present your offer can have a huge impact on the sale.

To the same point, the usual assumption is to bring in more revenue to go on sale or reduce costs to entice consumers, when actually putting the price up might be the answer.

Humans are irrational when it comes to the decision-making process and understanding the consumer psyche can be the answer to creating a value proposition or developing your product feature.

“Humans are incredibly bad at making decisions and are even worse at understanding what a product is truly worth.

Loads of companies have caught onto the idea that by using behavioural economic techniques they can increase their revenue by millions. Among others, Netflix uses a technique for their subscription service.

They give the consumer three options, 'Basic', 'Standard' and 'Premium', although 'Basic' is the cheapest, most people choose 'Standard'. 'Basic' is simply used as an upsell as nobody wants 'Basic' because it's, well, basic.

Humans are incredibly bad at making decisions and are even worse at understanding what a product is truly worth. Giving the consumer three options with names that trigger emotions can make those decisions easier.

They have no idea what the 'Basic' version is actually worth but they know they don't want basic, so they're left with 'Standard' and 'Premium'. If there were only two options, they would have nothing to compare either option to, but with three options and emotive names, option two and three are more appealing.

This is not a book on behavioural economics but in order to understand how to create great marketing campaigns that appeal to your audience you need to understand human behaviour.

Humans are the key to unlocking an incredible insight for your marketing, understanding them is your best chance of creating a campaign that catches on.

The biggest mistake most marketers make is assuming that all customers behave just like them and the truth is they're usually not. As Bob Hoffman simply puts it, 'Marketers Are From Mars, Consumers Are From New Jersey'.

If you haven't heard of Monzo bank, it's a new type of bank that has been labelled a 'challenger bank'. At the time they set the record for 'the quickest crowd-funding campaign in history' when they raised £1m in 96 seconds from the investment platform Crowdcube.

But that's another story, the more interesting story and one that was key to their success were their bank cards. They were a 'neon coral' colour. Now any research would tell them that nobody wanted a neon coral coloured card but people were instantly drawn to the eye-catching colour.

Although originally this neon coral card was used as a prototype, it has become a remarkable marketing tool, so they kept it. Human behaviour played a huge role in the success of Monzo, nobody could have predicted that a neon coral coloured card would be something consumers would be drawn to, but it was and still is.

They're the 'trendy bank' and when it comes to being trendy humans are drawn to being in the know, it's cool to be associated with them. The neon coral card is now so iconic to Monzo that they even tried to trademark the signature colour but failed.

Human behaviour is key to tapping into the certain quirks humans have, they're sometimes completely irrational but also obvious when done. Being the 'trendy bank' was key to Monzo's success but you can see how it could be easily transferred to another product or category.

Human behaviour is key to tapping into the certain quirks humans have.

Chapter 2: Ownable

Ownable is a hard thing to come by these days, most products and brands around now are almost identical.

Think about cars. The Kia has almost all the same bells and whistles as a BMW or Mercedes, but for a fraction of the price, you're literally just paying for the badge (and there's nothing wrong with that mind you).

So how does a brand own something when everyone is claiming the same thing?

Finding that one thing that your product does better than anyone else.

Apple is one of the best brands at doing this. They sell phones but focus their attention on just one feature of that phone that does it better than any other phone: their camera.

Their phones have some amazing features but they choose to only talk about the photos that your phone takes.

They have great apps, you can explore the internet from the palm of your hand, send emails, do work, read books, shop etc. but they never mention any of it because they know that every other smart phone can do those too. What they can't do is take photos like an iPhone can and even if they could, the Apple iPhone has now owned it and it's very hard for anyone else to claim it now even if their camera is better.

Back in the day Volvo 'owned' safety, people knew that if they bought a Volvo, they would have the safest car on the road. It was genius.

Then, one day, they decided to leave that message behind and sales started to decline. Throughout history many brands have abandoned the one thing they owned in that category — why?. Who knows, probably because a new marketing manager wanted to change something, but let's not speculate.

Ownable: The obsession with original ideas in advertising

Back in the day the idea of an 'original idea' was the holy grail in every advertising agency. Every creative person coming up with ideas would think, 'No, ditch that, that's been done before!'

Now, the concept of holding out every time for an original idea is simply, bloody stupid. Yet we as an industry are obsessed with 'original ideas'. Just look at the comments of our industry news and you'll see endless dismissive remarks like 'done before', 'not original' and so on.

OK. Ideas are what make the world go round, that and advertising (joking, not joking).

And love it or hate it, two of the biggest companies in the world, Google and Facebook, make most of their money off advertising.

Both companies were born from great ideas — a minimalist search engine and a place where we can connect with friends all over the world. But were they truly original? Most definitely not. Search engines that didn't actually work very well begat Google, which did. MySpace begat Facebook. In fact, sometimes the best ideas are those that have evolved, not 'original' ideas.

Take a look back in history — ideas are what have moved us forward, from the lightbulb to cars, these are things that have completely changed the way we live. But they are often derivations of what has gone before. Utterly original ideas are actually as rare as hens' teeth.

Let's look at other industries and compare. Science, for example, is made up of intellectual heroes building on someone's idea. They take previous studies and build on them. Expand on them. Build something fresh from what's gone before.

The music industry endlessly samples from generations past. Recording artists take something they love and build on it. Especially Hip-Hop; look at some of the great tracks of the last decade — most are samples from old soul music, reworked and brought up to date.

'Good artists borrow, great artists steal.'

– Banksy
– Steve Jobs
– Pablo Picasso

There's a great quote from Banksy. 'Good artists borrow, great artists steal.' He happened to steal that quote from Steve Jobs, who happened to steal the quote from Pablo Picasso, but you get the point.

Or Phillip Adams, a very original ad guy and now doyen of late-night 'brainfood' radio.

'Be smart: steal the good stuff.' What he said, right there.

Nothing is truly original. Everything that we do, hear, smell and watch is a product of the ideas that we produce from life experience. Everything comes from something, including the myriad creative inputs we all have. So why is it in advertising that there's this arrogant perception that everything we produce has to be original?

In advertising, there's no such thing as creative without strategy but if you're truly about getting results then why can't we adapt strategies that have been used and worked in the past?

OK, how we execute these strategies should be different, but it's more about taking what people have done in the past and building on it. Not ripping it off but making it your own or making it better. After all, the greatest artists in history studied at the feet of masters and then tried to emulate them, and then to enhance them.

Good work needs to be celebrated, wherever they came from. We need to stop pretending that we're all geniuses and start focusing on what's important, which is emphatically 'making money for our clients or brands'. We need to get our heads out of our arses and strive to make things better, and not necessarily obsess about being utterly original.

So, is originality bad? Of course not. It's just that it's not as important as results. If you can be utterly original AND effective, well bully for you. But businesses adopt ideas from other businesses all the time. People that work for those businesses aren't allowed to? Who made that rule into a commandment?

Whether that's an old strategy that's worked in the past or a YouTube video you've seen online, if it sells products and creates profits and jobs and positive change, does it matter where it came from? Really?

The point is owning something these days is almost impossible — but making something better isn't. Find that thing in your brand that you can own and make it better than anyone else.

"

Find that thing in your brand that you can own and make it better than anyone else.

“

Be single minded and your audience will single you out.

Ownable: Being single minded

According to BBH Labs the three greatest ads of all time are Guinness — 'Surfer', Nike — 'Just do it', and Apple — 'Think Different'.

We can debate BBH Labs' choice — and the most popular ad ever in the UK was recently judged to be a Hovis bread ad from thirty-plus years ago — but there are a few common threads with all these ads.

One is that they're all beautifully, thoughtfully, and intelligently written.

The other is that they are all beautifully produced.

The last — and probably most important common thread — is that they all have a clear USP — a unique selling proposition (or personality) — or SMP — single minded proposition — or whatever you prefer to call it.

Choose your own term. They all made it clear what they were all about. And they didn't cover it up with huge amounts of additional or extraneous information. One thing for sure, they all had a 'Hook'.

A book talking about the need for a USP? Really? Well, yes. You might think it's old hat, but it's one of the first things you learn as a trainee in advertising, and in recent years it seems that advertisers and their agencies seem to have somewhat misplaced this very simple mantra.

Just because it's been around awhile doesn't mean it still isn't 100% true. In fact, the term 'Unique Selling Proposition' actually dates back to a book published in 1961 called Reality in Advertising by Rosser Reeves and is still referred to today in universities around the world.

Reeves' world-changing idea was that the product or brand should show off the one reason it needed to be bought or how it was better than its competitors. Whether it was a slogan or brilliant copy, it focused on selling one unchallenged benefit. Just one.

What's more, it had to come from 'an insight' about the product or service, and the product or service itself had to be remarkable. The book also fiercely argued that the uniqueness of a brand/product can't just be made up from thin air as the consumer will eventually discover the deception, and sales will decrease.

In advertising agency parlance this thought was soon translated into the famous saying, 'You can sell any crap once'.

You can sell any crap once.

In other words, finding and promoting the USP wasn't some 'advertising gag' or trick, it was grounded in the reality of the marketplace.

The theory was also that swanky advertising for an average product would only increase the number of consumers disliking or bad-mouthing the brand.

Anyhow, Reeves' theory was extremely successful as demonstrated by a number of famous campaigns he created including 'Melt in your mouth, not in your hands' for M&Ms, 'It writes the first time, every time' for Bic Pens, and 'Fast, fast, fast relief' for Anacin headache remedy, to name just a few.

The issue these days is not that we've completely lost the understanding of the power of a unique selling proposition but that brands constantly want to change their brand expression, making it something new every year, and the USP can very easily get lost in that process.

But the theory was that once you have that 'one thing' it should not be changed willy-nilly but used over and over again until it sticks in consumers' minds like glue.

Apple is still remembered as the 'Think different' brand even though the campaign ran in 1989. As for 'Just do it', well, need I say more?

There is no doubt Reeves' theory is still relevant, and it works.

Being single-minded in anything you do is the easiest way to communicate and achieve results. (Not just in advertising but in life — and advertising should mimic life!)

Take the principle outside of the ad world.

Football greats dedicate their lives to one sport to achieve greatness. David Beckham, one of the most successful footballers of all time, used to stay on the pitch practising crossing the ball into the penalty area for hours after his teammates had gone to the showers.

Johnny Wilkinson, the greatest rugby dead-ball kicker of all time, did the same.

They didn't just one day decide they're going off to play hockey ... to give people a change. The reason? They were consistently giving people exactly what they wanted, advertised every week by their performances.

And they would probably suck at hockey.

So why then in advertising do we constantly need 'change'?

Creating a good campaign and sticking to it for years might just be the key to getting real market-changing results. Because creating and then sticking to your unique selling proposition gives you the upper hand against your competitors.

Creating a good campaign and sticking to it for years might just be the key to getting real market-changing results.

Why do we forget this simple truth? Well, a lot of today's marketing failures are about chasing short term sales to the detriment of a brand's carefully considered positioning. Never a good idea.

So find your unique selling proposition and stick to it, it may take longer to see the results but when you do, your brand will be 'unique'. And if you're not sure what your USP is, well, start by working that out. That will be your 'Hook'.

Embrace your uniqueness, people will find it attractive.

Ownable: Craft

Craft is what makes ads remarkable, it's what we see on display every award season and is what makes advertising messages worth watching, it can even make your ad ownable.

It's the difference between something average and something great. We've all seen great ideas crafted really badly, and bad ideas crafted well, and it makes a huge difference.

The thing is that today we have this thing called social media where there's a constant need to produce endless amounts of 'stuff' — what I like to call the 'C word', and what others like to call 'Content'.

Whatever the medium, great ads are fewer and further between these days because they cost money and time — and they need to be created by minds who are obsessed with creating big ideas and then crafting them.

And that ain't the case with most content.

When you break it down, 'content' is just advertising ... you can call it whatever you like but it's still bloody advertising. And as more and more clients are now doing their own advertising — and calling it 'content' — the question really has to be asked, 'What's the value of an idea anymore?'

And then, close on the heels of that question, 'Does craft even exist anymore?'

The answer to the C word is simple: all brands, no matter how big or small, need (and should value) an outside view and they need it for their content flow as much as anything else. (And frankly, if the wilder predictions for the influence of social media are anything like true — we doubt it, but if they are — then they especially need those external eyes on their social media.)

It's called perspective. Fresh eyes. Over the years we've all seen a few brands take all their marketing/ advertising in-house and in many cases it has failed. (*Cough* Pepsi, anyone?)

If you think your in-house graphic artists in their cubicle are ever going to offer you something that will change the minds of millions of people, then frankly you're deluding yourself. It's not what they do, and it's not what they should be asked to do.

People need to refocus. The only reason you advertise is so that you can stand out, but if brands don't value an idea — and the craft to make it shine and scintillate — then they won't stand out, and we're all doomed and there's no rainbows, sunshine or unicorns for anyone, and especially for the clients that killed them.

The industry loves the idea of things being 'dead', TV is 'dead', digital is 'dead', but when it comes to 'craft', there's a strange feeling that it is, at least, dying. Or at least, it is not appreciated like it used to be.

Think of a brilliant 'theatre of the mind' radio ad. How many of those are on air nowadays? Precious few.

So the question at hand is actually the whole state of advertising, where we're at and where we're going. Yes, there's tech this and data that, but let's be real here: our industry makes ads — that's what we do — and what platform they sit on isn't an idea, it's just a delivery mechanism.

There's no such thing as digital advertising or even digital strategy, there's just good advertising and bad advertising. Whether it's VR, AR or whatever the next trendy buzz word is, it's still advertising. These are not ideas in themselves, these are platforms for ideas. There's a big difference, and crafting these ideas needs time, money and top creative talent to make them great and ownable.

As mentioned earlier, advertising should be thought of as entertainment, because if we don't entertain then we lose and there's no point. We interrupt people's lives, that's what we do, so if we're going to do that we may as well entertain them. And in order to do that we need to craft that idea until it's something the brand can own.

Craft is what makes things ownable, so stop and make time for your communication to be crafted until it represents something you can own.

“

Craft is what makes things ownable, so stop and make time for your communication to be crafted until it represents something you can own.

Chapter 3: Offer

In marketing, your offer is one of the most important aspects of your brand. It's closely linked to 'ownable' but can be done in a number of ways. An offer can be the heart of your brand or this week's special.

Purpose driven advertising came to light in 2016 and really ramped up in 2019. What your brand offers and trying to do good in the world are two very different things.

If your offer is driven by your core values as a brand it's fine, but if you're trying to force a charitable thing on people, they'll smell it from a mile away. It has to always come from what your company offers or stands for.

In 2004, a campaign was launched that offered the idea of 'real beauty', something that wasn't really in the marketing space. Most beauty brands focused on highly retouched images of beautiful women. After loads of research, they decided to offer a different side of beauty.

The story goes that Ogilvy, the agency responsible for creating the real beauty campaign, created a film called 'Daughters' that centred around young girls and the issues they face with beauty at school and with peers as they grow up. It was a long form interview style film that would be hosted on the real beauty website.

An offer can be the heart of your brand or this week's special.

It was nicely produced and offered the viewer a different side of the beauty industry.

It was Art Director Tim Piper who had the idea to use the leftover money from the film to make an ad. It instantly went viral and now has over 20 million views on YouTube.

The point is Dove offered women something entirely different to what they're used to seeing in the beauty industry and they continue to use this strategy today, over 15 years later.

“

An offer comes in many forms and it’s up to you to decide the differences between your brand offer and your day-to-day offer.

Whether it's '1000 songs in your pocket' (iPod) or more recently 'Shot on an iPhone' (iPhone), Apple is king at this technique.

They understand the consumer and their low attention span, they know if they focus their offer on one product benefit they have more chance at standing out. And that's advertising, being single-minded and making sure your offer is solid.

An offer comes in many forms and it's up to you to decide the differences between your brand offer and your day-to-day offer. There's a big difference but if you can align them both it's even better.

IKEA has their offer sorted. They are unique in their offering, in brand and in retail. Over the years they've been mostly consistent in all their offerings.

Firstly, they started with a psychological insight into human behaviour. It's been proven that people are more satisfied once they've built something themselves.

That in itself is an amazing offering but IKEA goes further than that. Whether it's their brand advertising or their retail advertising they are very clear what they offer.

Their spot called 'Lamp' was one of those ads that you could almost call perfect.

It opens with a shot of a red lamp. A woman unplugs it and proceeds to carry it outside. We then see it from the lamp's point of view. The woman leaves the lamp outside on the footpath. A slow and sad piano piece plays in the background as the lamp sits alone through wind and rain. The lamp looks up at the window and sees it's been replaced.

This goes on for some time and then a man steps into frame and says to the camera, 'Many of you feel bad for this lamp. That is because you crazy [sic]. It has no feelings, and the new one is much better.'

The commercial ends with the IKEA logo above the campaign's tagline 'Unböring', and a link to its website, Unböring.com.

The commercial offers the viewer a number of things, but besides being a great piece of film, directed by one of the great directors of our time, Spike Jones, it tells the audience that Ikea is very single minded in its offering.

You can sell many products but as mentioned earlier being single minded in your approach can be a powerful tool in getting people's attention. The default is to try and tell your audience that you offer everything, when sometimes it's best to tell people you sell lamps. Just saying.

“The default is to try and tell your audience that you offer everything, when sometimes it’s best to tell people you sell lamps.

Offer: What's the purpose of brand purpose?

The first purpose of advertising is to grab the audience's attention.

That's it. Nothing more, nothing less. Because if your ads aren't noticed, nothing else matters. Game over, right there.

Beyond that, though, great advertising comes from either an insight into your product/ brand or insight into your target market.

The 2018 Gillette ad is a perfect example of the latter.

In the commercial starts with a number of men looking in the mirror with quick cut news reporters speaking of 'bullying', 'the Me Too movement', 'sexual harassment' and 'toxic masculinity'. Then a male voiceover begins, 'Is this the best a man can get?'

What we must remember is that unlike those who toil away in the marketing industry, or who are paid to comment on popular culture, the consumer really does not care about the convoluted discussions.

People don't pull apart advertising and deconstruct every word as we do.

People don't pull apart advertising and deconstruct every word as we do.

They were basically addressing the sign of the times and some felt it was trying to capitalise on this. And maybe they were, but it's up to the consumer to decide that.

Gillette has long sought to 'own' masculinity — the essence of what it means to be a man — and they did just that in a spot that caused debate in the marketing industry and media.

They simply watch, maybe have a fleeting opinion then move on to the next thing. They may, or may not, have learned something which they will use in the future, consciously or subconsciously.

A study by Nielsen's Global Trust in Advertising report showed that despite this very obvious truth, 75% of consumers worldwide expect brands to contribute to their well-being and quality of life. And this notion of what has been called 'brand purpose' is especially important when marketing to millennials, 71% of whom say they prefer brands that drive social and environmental change.

Now, brand purpose can mean a lot of different things. You can have brand purpose directly from a product — a better mousetrap — but you can also stand for something bigger as a brand.

What you seek to express as a purpose needs to mesh with who you really are as a brand.

What you seek to express as a purpose needs to mesh with who you really are as a brand. This is where it gets tricky, of course. Whatever a brand aligns itself with — social issues, environmental issues etc. — should also align closely with what you can own as a company.

Because for a generation Gillette has owned masculinity — the best a man can get, anyone? — their 'The Best Men Can Be' commercial is just fine. Whether you like the spot or not, it aligns with what they have always stood for — an image of what men should be.

The same goes for Nike and their 'Dream Crazy' commercial — this is perfectly aligned with everything Nike has always stood for.

Of course, the conversation gets much more complicated when you think about whether 'brand purpose' is everything about you — it's not just external, it's internal, it's what your company wants to stand for.

One criticism of the Gillette spot, for example, was that Gillette is owned by Procter and Gamble, which also makes skin lightening and whitening creams sold to millions in Asia and the Middle East, and that it's inherently racist to tell dark women — it's always women — that they are not OK looking the way they were born, and that P&G, therefore, perpetuate ridiculous and homogeneous beauty standards to make money.

Of course, the conversation gets much more complicated when you think about whether 'brand purpose' is everything about you — it's not just external, it's internal, it's what your company wants to stand for.

One criticism of the Gillette spot, for example, was that Gillette is owned by Procter and Gamble, which also makes skin lightening and whitening creams sold to millions in Asia and the Middle East, and that it's inherently racist to tell dark women — it's always women — that they are not OK looking the way they were born, and that P&G, therefore, perpetuate ridiculous and homogeneous beauty standards to make money.

So we should always remember that when we stick our heads above the parapet they can get shot off, too.

There have been numerous examples of companies seeking to appear environmentally aware only to be pulled up for not adhering to decent environmental standards in their real-world behaviour and accused of 'greenwashing'.

So we should always remember that when we stick our heads above the parapet they can get shot off, too.

There have been numerous examples of companies seeking to appear environmentally aware only to be pulled up for not adhering to decent environmental standards in their real-world behaviour and accused of 'greenwashing'.

But we can't ignore brand purpose just because it's tricky.

As a colleague said to me once, 'your brand is actually what people say about you when you leave the room'. This sums up the whole brand purpose discussion perfectly. If you can add purpose to your brand that makes people discuss it positively when you leave the room, then you're being smart.

Increasingly we choose to buy products not for what they are but what they mean to us.

Ultimately, you see, it's about trust. If we trust someone, we're almost certainly going to say or think good things about them. Increasingly we choose to buy products not for what they are but what they mean to us. If they align with our beliefs or values then we'll be more likely to buy them.

No wonder brand purpose fascinates marketers.

Of course, brand purpose isn't a 'new' thing, it's always been there. We just have a new name for it now.

Nike is a perfect example. Nike sells shoes but they actually stand for something way bigger than that. They stand for effort.

Apple sells phones, watches, computers (and music!) but they have creativity as their bigger purpose.

Even brands like Toms Shoes and Thank You personal care are doing great things with a bigger purpose.

The point is to make sure your brand's higher purpose is aligned with what you truly stand for as a brand.

So what do you offer? Really offer? More and more it looks like it's worth spending the time to work that out. And then tell people.

“

Give your audience something they’ll never forget and they’ll repay you forever.

Offer: Beyond the offer

Your offer has to be backed up. Once you hook your customer you have to back up that offer with service, understanding their needs and offering support.

Disney is a great example of a complete offering, everything they do, sell and make is magical.

Their offering begins with the theme parks, everything about the place is magical. You see, staff members at Disneyland aren't really staff, they're 'cast members'. Every employee in the park, whether they are operating the rides, serving food or performing, are called Cast Members.

This alone sets the tone of the theme park, it's a stage, and therefore as a Cast Member you're part of the act. You have to stay in character at all times and you're not allowed to reference anything outside the Disney Universe.

Now, this may seem extreme to some but it shows Disney's commitment to their offering goes well beyond the consumer. Their offering is part of the company and the employees all buy into that.

Coming back to your product is also very important. In 2020, Tesco offered consumers something that nobody had really even asked for, well not nobody, specifically one person via a tweet.

In fact, it was one of Tesco's employees that noticed a tweet that went viral, from Dominique Apollon who stated his lifelong search for a bandage that matched his skin tone.

An offer can come in many shapes and sizes, sometimes it's this week's sale and other times it's a completely new product.

Tesco went on to design bandages in a range of tones along with a series of ads that were equally as smart and it was an instant success. The fact that no one had offered it before is amazing but it shows that your offers can come from anywhere and sometimes it's not an ad but a twist on your product offering.

The point is, an offer can come in many shapes and sizes, sometimes it's this week's sale and other times it's a completely new product.

In Tesco's case they made themselves a completely new offer that had never existed before. For large organisations this can be rare, in most cases innovations come from startups because in large organisations they're mostly stuck in their ways with statements like 'we've always done it like this', hence nothing changes. Tesco has an outlier and their new bandage offering is a game changer.

For a brand like Elastoplast, Tesco offering this new line of bandages would be infuriating. They would be scrambling to bring their own range of bandage tones to market ASAP. I guarantee by the time this book comes out they'll already have a range in the market.

Chapter 4: Keep

This is the one all marketers live for. That one liner or visual that people talk about for years to come.

We forget that what we advertise isn't just some special esoteric thing called an ad, it's a message ... a message from someone's business to our head. And like all good messages, that message should be spreadable.

When we were all in school, we'd hear a story or a joke and then tell that story/joke to a friend and then it would spread. Soon enough everyone in the school would know it, then the school in the next suburb would know it, and so on and so on. The same with great songs, an amazing TV show or brilliant advertising.

We forget that what we advertise isn't just some special esoteric thing called an ad, it's a message ... a message from someone's business to our head.

Whatever the platform or media is, that's not how things spread. It's the consumer that spreads the message ...

Things went viral way before the internet. We've all heard the saying 'An apple a day keeps the doctor away', right? Well, it dates back to the 1860s in Wales.

Working people had poor diets and were especially lacking in vitamin C, but apples were cheap and plentiful. The phrase is one of the first examples of social advertising in history.

The original saying was actually 'Eat an apple on going to bed, and you'll keep the doctor from earning his bread'. Over the years it evolved to 'An apple a day, no doctor to pay' or 'An apple a day sends the doctor away'. The meaning and message are just as relevant today. Because it has real value.

The message came from a truth and so it stuck — and it spread far and wide, and still does.

In the 1860s they didn't have Twitter, Facebook, Instagram, TikTok and all the rest — just plain old people spreading the good oil.

The point is, whatever the platform or media is, that's not how things spread. It's the consumer that spreads the message, so the message needs to be based on a consumer value, and it needs to be really good, catchy and have a hook.

One way to get this invaluable 'talkability' happening is by making ads that get the attention of mainstream media — ads that get commented on. This is one key to successfully spreading your message.

The more people that see it the more likely it is to move into culture. But how often does a brief to an ad agency start with the words: 'I want this ad to be talked about!'

Ads can be shocking, funny or heartfelt. Whatever technique is used, they must be good.

Relevant.
Entertaining.
Thought-provoking.
Moving.

Whether it's 'an apple a day' or 'Finger lickn' good', if it's good, people will talk about it.

When it's obviously a great idea, people want to be part of it. Whether it's a phrase, a TV commercial, or a much-needed social change, you have to ask two questions: what's in it for the consumer, and have we communicated that as brilliantly as we can? Every time.

And sometimes it's really not as hard as we seem to make it.

> **'Your message spreads from human mind to human mind, to human mind.'**
>
> – David Trott

Things that rhyme are proven to be catchier in people's minds, for example. So, if you're a parent and you want your child to be healthy, 'An apple a day, keeps the doctor away' is an easy way to convince your child to 'buy' the idea of eating a piece of fruit. That's why jingles always used to be a common component of great ads. But today?

Most young copywriters have never even written a jingle.

The lesson? Customers hold the key to helping a brand grow and getting a brand's message out there. Without getting them onside, it's very hard to be truly successful. Marketers need to remember this when something is presented to them.

As mentioned earlier, and as David Trott said it best, your message spreads: 'From human mind to human mind, to human mind.'

People will forget what you did, but people will never forget how you made them feel.

Keep: Theatre of the mind

Like most folklore, I'm sure this story has been told many times, in many different ways.

In the early '90s in London, all the hot agencies were pitching for a dream client.

All but one had done their tap dance to show that they were the agency to take the client forward.

The clients came to the final agency to hear what they had to say. They walked through the doors into the foyer and approached the front desk. The CEO said to the receptionist, 'We're from Transport for London, we have a meeting at 10 am'. The receptionist replied calmly, 'Yes, please take a seat, they're expecting you'.

So the crew of six-odd clients took their seats in the foyer and waited to be taken through.

Five minutes went by and no one came. Ten minutes went by and still, no one came.

Fifteen minutes went by and eventually the CEO got up and asked the receptionist what on earth was going on. She smiled and said, 'Yes, they won't be a moment, please take a seat, someone will be with you shortly'.

So, the CEO sat back down and ensured his colleagues that he'd been told that it won't be much longer. They all smiled and relaxed.

Twenty minutes went by and still no one came. By this time the CEO and his staff were feeling very agitated.

Finally, after thirty-odd minutes of sitting in the foyer, the CEO marched up to the receptionist and demanded that someone come and get them to have the presentation or else they'll leave and won't have any chance of having them as a client.

The receptionist looked at the CEO, smiled and said, 'Yes I understand your frustration but please take a seat, someone is coming to take you through shortly'. At this point the CEO was furious, to the point that he said, 'Fine that's it, we're leaving!' and began to walk his staff out of the agency.

At that exact moment, the Creative Director came through the door and said 'Now you know what it feels like for the commuters waiting for your trains and buses, every day'.

The CEO and his staff stood there stunned by his comment. The agency apparently went on to do their pitch and won the client.

The point of this theatre was to show the client they understood the business and frustrations of their clientele. But more importantly, they showed the client something no other agency had done, they created a scenario in the client's mind, a theatre that was easily relatable.

Theatre of the mind is often related to radio advertising but it can be used in so many situations, even in movies.

For instance, in *Reservoir Dogs* when Mr Blonde cuts the cop's ear off, you never actually see the ear getting cut off but the audience remembers it as if they had. Or the scene in *Psycho* where Lila gets stabbed in the shower.

Theatre plays a huge role in all aspects of advertising and we need to bring it back. Theatre of the mind is what makes people talk about the ad, movie or song. If there's a picture in their mind, they're more likely to keep it with them for the rest of their lives.

If you look at some of the greatest films, TV shows, songs or commercials, they all had something that left you wanting to tell people. They're usually simple, have strong emotive storylines and offer the audience a reason to keep it with them.

If there's a picture in their mind, they're more likely to keep it with them for the rest of their lives.

“

First, make an impression. Second, leave an impression.

Keep: Word of mouth

As mentioned earlier in this chapter, people are key to helping your message spread so word of mouth is your tool.

Word of mouth is one of the oldest forms of marketing, it's been around since cavemen times. Cavemen would tell their tribe where the best hunting areas were and others would then follow suit.

Although social media has potentially made it easier to help things spread, it's not the reason things spread. 'Likes' can only take you so far and people are not trusting social media like they used to.

In order to get your audience to spread your message, campaign or idea you have to use human insights, an offer, something that you can own or all of the above.

Whether it's your great service, your remarkable product or just an incredible story, you need to give them a reason to talk about you.

When people relay a story, they don't detail every part word by word, they make it their own.

Psychology plays a huge role in people spreading your message. If your story makes them look cool, interesting, in-the-know or smart, they are more than likely to tell that story.

When people relay a story, they don't detail every part word by word, they make it their own. They make it sound like it happened to them.

The key is giving people no choice but to talk about your brand, message or product.

In February 2018, Elon Musk did exactly that. He decided to launch the 'Tesla Roadster', an electric sports car, into space. It was even equipped with a mannequin dressed in a spacesuit sitting in the driver's seat.

It was the first and only production car in space, making it a very talkable stunt.

Elon Musk is known for not really doing advertising but having said that, launching a car into space might just be the most expensive ad of all time.

Live video was transmitted for slightly over four hours, although some thought the stunt was extreme and would contribute to space debris, there was no doubt that it was one to remember.

Red Bull uses a very similar strategy. In October 2012 they set out to break a record held by Joseph Kittinger for 62 years.

The energy drink giant did something that will be talked about for years to come. The stunt, called 'Red Bull Stratos', saw Austrian skydiver Felix Baumgartner fly into the stratosphere over New Mexico in a helium balloon and free fall from space.

The jump itself lasted about 10 minutes and broke a number of records along the way but will be talked about for decades to come.

Footage was, of course, streamed on YouTube with cameras and GoPros so the audience could see every moment. The genius though was that Red Bull made sure the focus was on breaking the record and not on the brand, they wanted to get their audience to focus on pushing the boundaries of what is humanly possible.

They played the side act. Science and engineering were the main act. And it worked.

The stunt was viewed on nearly 80 TV stations in 50 countries, not to mention the digital views, with YouTube racking in 8 million live streams and clocking over 45 million views on the Red Bull channel alone.

“

Find that narrative, break a record or tell an incredible story and you’ll have that message spread like wildfire.

These are obviously very expensive examples but the idea was what made them spread. They had a remarkable word of mouth effect, people wanted to tell others what they had just witnessed.

Word of mouth is one of the oldest forms of marketing but also the most effective when you nail it. Find that narrative, break a record or tell an incredible story and you'll have that message spread like wildfire.

‘HOOK’ theory only works if you know these 5 principles

1. Know your target market.

OK, this might seem like a 'No sh*t Sherlock' moment — too obvious to be worth saying — but you need to really look at who you're talking to. Not just what type of things they read, watch and listen to, but when, and why. What is their mood when they see your ad? What are they doing when your ad interrupts their lives?

Look very closely at the age of your preferred target market because this will determine the type of advertising or medium you might choose to use. For example, if it's dentures you're selling, social media might not be the place to advertise, even if it looks affordable at first glance! Be as specific as you can be.

If you're a 50-year-old business-person who is selling a product or service to 'young people', you might think that 18-year-olds and 25-year-olds are pretty much the same. Well, they're not.

Unless your product literally appeals to everybody (and that's a very rare thing) you need to put yourself in your desired customer's shoes.

We're in the business of psychology: what does your target think, what type of person are they? How do they like to receive information? What tone works best with them?

Think long and hard about this, and then — and only then — do an advertisement. There are now so many different types of mediums to advertise on; pick the one that suits your target and then dominate it so there is no chance they will miss your message.

Be as specific as you can be.

2. Make sure your product is remarkable.

This should be the first rule. In such a cluttered marketplace, if your product isn't good then you won't sell anything, no matter how much you advertise. We have a well-worn saying in our business: 'You can sell any rubbish. Once.' Consumers are much more demanding nowadays, and there's plenty of competition around that allows them to choose good quality.

The better your product is, the more people will talk about it and the more people will buy it.

There's no doubt advertising works — without it nobody would know you even exist — but if you do get someone to buy your product and it's no good then he/she will simply tell their friends and then you won't sell any more product. We call this 'social currency' and you need as much of it as the real stuff.

Similarly, the better your product is, the more people will talk about it and the more people will buy it.

Think about the blockbuster TV show *Game of Thrones* — you probably heard a friend talking about it, then another, then another, until you just had to see what all the fuss was about, and the rest is history.

So before you do anything, ask yourself, 'Is my product amazing?' If it isn't amazing, work on making it so before you tell the world about it.

3. Know your product benefit.

Know what your product offers your consumer, how it can truly benefit them. What it means for consumers' lives and their sense of well-being.

This is really important as it will guide what you say in your advertising. It will help you stand out from the crowd and stand out from your potential competitors.

Find the one thing that differentiates your brand from another.

Sometimes people concentrate on selling the features of their product or service but forget to translate that into hard benefits for their customers. Sometimes we need to draw that conclusion for people who are time poor, and who aren't looking at our offering with the same obsession that we are!

Let's look at a product that changed people's leisure time forever.

When the Apple iPod launched, the advertising campaign was incredibly simple. It told consumers a truth and something that was simply amazing — unheard of — about the product: '1000 songs in your pocket'.

The customer benefit was obvious — more music available, instantly, than ever before! When you think about the time the iPod was released people were using Discmans and had to carry CDs around with them.

To tell people that they could now have 1000 songs in their pocket, well, it really was remarkable. (Note: I put amazing in italics to refer you back to our second point.

Amazing is what you need to be aiming for!)

So find the one thing that differentiates your brand from another. Ad agencies call it the 'Single Minded Proposition'. This will help you to understand what you should be saying.

If your product or service really is amazing then there are two ways to look at advertising — either an insight about what makes the product so unusual and brilliant, or an insight about the target audience and how it will help them. Sometimes that's one and the same — given a choice, the latter is always the most powerful way to go.

4. People honestly don’t care about your brand.

There's a line from one of the greatest ad men that ever lived, David Ogilvy, that sums it up: 'You aren't advertising to a standing army — you are advertising to a moving parade.'

What he meant by that is that people are just too busy, getting groceries, picking up the kids, going to the movies, eating a meal ... whatever it is, people are always moving ... and are not obsessively interested in what you have to say. They don't stand still and pay attention. So, whatever you say, it had better be immediately compelling and interesting.

Nobody really cares about your brand as much as you do. That's hard to take, we know, but it's true. Once you come to terms with that statement it makes life a lot easier to advertise and a lot easier to know what you have to do to stand out.

Consumers will simply never love your brand as much as you do. Think about it like a photo of your child: you think they look super cute, it's just the random person you're showing who doesn't really care.

Does this mean branding doesn't matter? Not at all! It does, in many ways. It simply means you cannot assume that consumers have digested all your careful brand strategy and all the features of your brand that you agonise over all day, every day.

They don't go to bed thinking, 'I must get some brand X tomorrow'. Whereas you go to bed thinking, 'I must sell some more brand X tomorrow'. Understanding that difference is a key factor in crafting messages that will really resonate with your audience.

People are always moving ... and are not obsessively interested in what you have to say.

5. Simplify your message. Edit, edit, edit.

Consumers are busy and they generally don't have the time — or care enough — to carefully read, watch or listen to your ad. So, make your ad as simple as possible.

Consumers are faced with thousands of ads a day, so for your ad to stand out in the crowd, you need them to 'get' your message as quickly as possible. There are a few rules in advertising that are worth following: a billboard should consist of no more than eight words; and a TV or social film should grab your attention within the first three seconds, or better yet, the first frame! A print ad in the newspaper has less than 0.2 seconds to seize the readers' attention before they move on, so you'd better have a great headline or a very powerful picture.

Keep it simple, stupid.

(There's a reason for that eight words on a billboard, by the way. It's not just that people are driving past at speed and are quite rightly concentrating on the road. It's also because eight seconds is the limit of human short-term memory. There is a bit of science to advertising sometimes!)

Always remember to obey the KISS principle: Keep it simple, stupid. It's a great reminder that whatever you're doing remember to keep the message easy to digest so your audience can both understand it and remember you amongst the clutter.

Conclusion

As you have read in this book, there is no simple way for your communications to 'go viral'. A lot of the time it's a bit of luck and helped with a bit of money but using the 'Hook' theory will hopefully give your marketing the ingredients to help it in the right direction.

In 2010 a video was posted on YouTube, along with hundreds of thousands of other videos that day.

It was uploaded by Paul Vasquez, whose YouTube channel was Hungrybear9562. It featured a very emotional Paul filming and describing a rainbow that then turns into a double rainbow.

The very emotional Paul describes the rainbow for over three minutes. The video sat there quietly on YouTube for around six months until 3 July 2010 when comedian and late-night talk show host Jimmy Kimmel decided to tweet the video to his millions of followers, describing it as 'the funniest video in the world'.

The rest is history.

Celebrities can be a huge influence when it comes to things 'going viral'.

The point is, this was a unique film, but it was literally not known until a very famous Jimmy Kimmel made it famous. Double rainbow is now used in pop culture around the world but sometimes things need a little nudge — or in this case a huge nudge — to get going.

Celebrities can be a huge influence when it comes to things 'going viral'.

In the case of Paul Vasquez's Double Rainbow video, it still had a hook though. It was very human, offered the audience something unique and it was very ownable to Paul, nobody but him could have made that video. And last, it gave the viewer something to keep and talk to their friends about with two simple words 'Double Rainbow'.

You see, hooks live in all assets of life, they're common. Creating them might be hard but not impossible.

As there's no guarantees in making your campaign catch on, Hook theory will hopefully give you the best chance going forward.

“

Stand for something, then walk it.

Human

Human emotion is a powerful tool when it comes to communications and storytelling. Make sure there's a human truth to the campaign or idea. People are the ones that spread the word or make things 'go viral', so make sure you have tapped into a human insight.

Ownable

Is the strategy ownable? It doesn't have to be completely original but something your brand can own. You can have the same strategy as someone else but make sure you do it better.

Offer

What are you offering your audience? What's in it for them? Give your audience something: it could be a discount or competition, make them feel good or laugh, as long as you give them something they can take away, it's job done.

Keep

Will they remember it, keep it with them and pass it on? A good idea will stay with someone and it will be spreadable if it has a hook. Give them something to talk about — remember that TV show you loved and told everyone about? The same applies in marketing. People want to be entertained.

Thank you.

Thanks to think different.

Thanks to just do it.

Thanks to we try harder.

Thanks to impossible is nothing.

Thanks to taste the rainbow.

Thanks to obey your thirst.

Thanks to Wassup?!

Thanks to the man your man could smell like.

Thanks to dumb ways to die.

Thanks to it's a big ad.

Thanks to fearless girl.

Thanks to colour like no other.

Thanks to real beauty.

Again, I want to thank my wife and everyone that's made this happen. That includes Wilkinson Publishing for taking the leap of faith. Everyone that I've learnt from over the years. Most of all, everyone that took a risk on me.

Thanks to all the clients that approved the crazy ideas that I came up with and ran with it, you'll know who you are.

Weirdly, thanks to COVID lockdown for allowing me to put this book together.

Thanks to all the copywriters I've worked with as I've learnt something from each of you, again you know who you are.

Thanks to my parents for always supporting me, especially when I was younger and had a lot of learning difficulties.

Last of all, thank you for reading.

Not goodbye, see you later.

About the author:

Pat Langton has been in the advertising business for over 20 years.

He's worked in London and is now based in Melbourne.

He's picked up a number of international advertising awards including a Cannes Lion and Clio to name a few.

Get in touch:

readhookbook.com

@readhookbook

@readhookbook

@patlangton

linkedin.com/pat-langton

About the designer:

As above.